Workbook for
The Study of
Orchestration
Fourth Edition

Workbook for
The Study of
Orchestration

Fourth Edition

Samuel Adler

Professor Emeritus, Eastman School of Music of the University of Rochester
Composition Faculty, Juilliard School of Music

W. W. Norton and Company
New York · London

W. W. Norton & Company has been independent since its founding in 1923, when William Warder Norton and Mary D. Herter Norton first began publishing lectures delivered at the People's Institute, the adult education division of New York City's Cooper Union. The Nortons soon expanded their program beyond the institute, publishing books by celebrated academics from America and abroad. By mid-century, the two major pillars of Norton's publishing program—trade books and college texts—were firmly established. In the 1950s, the Norton family transferred control of the company to its employees, and today—with a staff of four hundred and a comparable number of trade, college, and professional titles published each year—W. W. Norton & Company stands as the largest and oldest publishing house owned wholly by its employees.

Editor: Justin Hoffman
Project Editor: David Bradley
Editorial Assistant: Grant Phelps
Managing Editor, College: Marian Johnson
Managing Editor, College Digital Media: Kim Yi
Production Manager: Andy Ensor
Composition: Graphic World
Manufacturing: Sheridan Books, Inc.

Permission to use copyrighted material is included on page 239.

ISBN 978-0-393-28317-4

W. W. Norton & Company, Inc., 500 Fifth Avenue, New York, NY 10110
wwnorton.com

W. W. Norton & Company, Ltd., Castle House, 15 Carlisle Street, London W1D 3BS

67890

Contents

Preface

I am delighted by the response I have received for the Workbook for *The Study of Orchestration*. Like the workbook for the third edition, this workbook contains the following exercises designed to reinforce what students read in the textbook and help them learn how to orchestrate:

- **Test Yourself** activities gauge students' comprehension of key concepts from the text.

- **Worksheets** provide opportunities to practice orchestrating short passages.

- **Listen and Score** activities ask students to identify instrumentation aurally and notate it.

Building on the workbook's success, I have expanded the number of choices of works to be orchestrated. While the workbook includes more orchestration exercises than could be used in any single class, the variety of works gives the instructor an opportunity to select works that are ideal for a class or assign each student a different work so as to make the experience richer for the class. These excerpts will expose the students to a larger repertory and challenge their imagination since many more styles from various periods are represented. While some of the exercises are quite long, I suggest that only portions of them may be assigned, especially for beginning students. I strongly suggest that, if at all possible, live performances of student works are crucial for the orchestrator.

With this new edition, I have also added additional easy exercises—particularly Listen and Score exercises—to make the workbook accessible to a wide range of students. These exercises feature a variety of instrumental ensembles; in particular, I have emphasized works for band. For me, orchestration is about ear training. Therefore, I feel that the assignment of the Listen and Score exercises is of the utmost importance even if the orchestration course is only a single term.

Since this project is a very sizable one, there are always errors that, even though rather small, need to be corrected. I wish to acknowledge the tremendous help in trying to make the new edition as error-free as possible. To this end, I had the invaluable help of Professor David Schober of the Aaron Copland School of Music and I am ever so grateful to him for his devotion to this project.

Samuel Adler
March 2016

Workbook for
The Study of
Orchestration
Fourth Edition

Test Yourself I

Strings

1. Name the open strings on each instrument:

    a. violin _____

    b. viola _____

    c. cello _____

    d. double bass _____

2. What is the meaning of *sul D*? _____

3. What is the III string on the viola? _____

4. What is the I string on the double bass?

5. What is the II string on the cello? _____

6. What is the IV string on the violin? _____

7. What is meant by *scordatura*? _____

    Give an example. _____

8. What is meant by third position on the violin? _____

_____

_____

_____

9. What is a double stop? _____

_____

10. Why are the following double stops not possible to perform on each designated instrument?

_____

_____

Violin   **Cello**   **Viola**

11. Here is a chord progression from Mozart's *Le Nozze di Figaro*. Expand each simple chord into one using double, triple, or quadruple stops for each section of strings. Write triple stops in all places unless otherwise specified (②= double stop; ④ = quadruple stop). Leave the double-bass line as single notes, except for the last chord. The first chord is given.

    Adagio

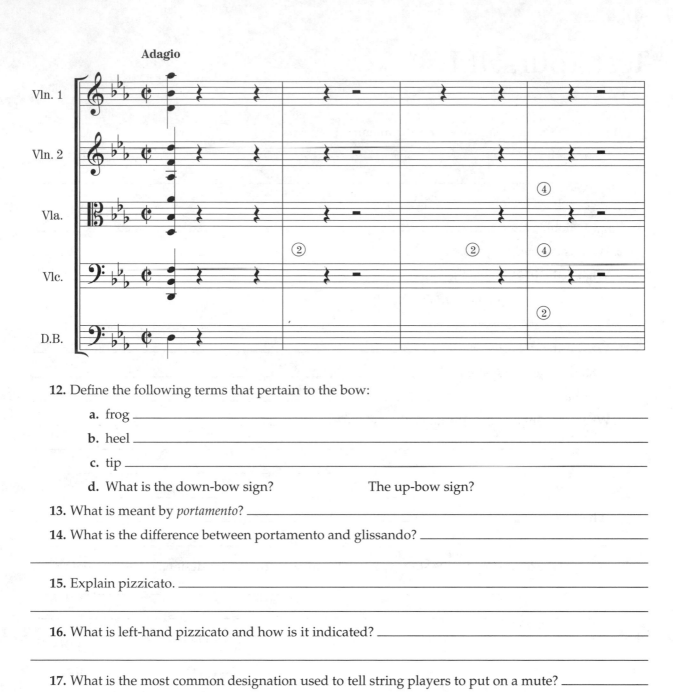

12. Define the following terms that pertain to the bow:

    a. frog _____

    b. heel _____

    c. tip _____

    d. What is the down-bow sign?   The up-bow sign?

13. What is meant by *portamento*? _____

14. What is the difference between portamento and glissando? _____

_____

15. Explain pizzicato. _____

_____

16. What is left-hand pizzicato and how is it indicated? _____

_____

17. What is the most common designation used to tell string players to put on a mute? _____

_____

18. To take off the mute? _____

19. What is a natural harmonic? _____

_____

_____

20. Write two natural harmonics for each of the four bowed string instruments. (Write both the correct notation and what the actual sound will be.)

21. What is an artificial harmonic? _____

_____

22. Write three artificial harmonics for each of the following: violin, viola, and cello. (Write both the correct notation and what the actual sound will be.)

23. Describe the difference between the way an artificial harmonic is produced on the violin and on

the cello. _____

_____

_____

24. What is meant by *harmonic series?* _____

_____

25. Write out the first six overtones for the following fundamentals:

a.   b.   c.

Worksheet 1

Clefs

1. Rewrite for viola in alto clef.

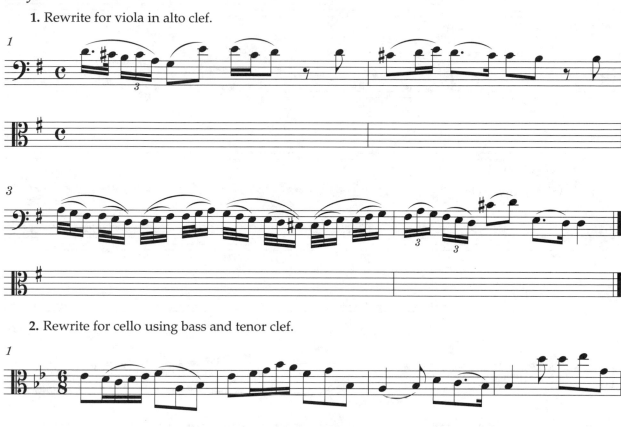

2. Rewrite for cello using bass and tenor clef.

3. Rewrite in alto clef.

4. Rewrite in treble clef.

5. Transcribe for viola (include bowings).

6. Transcribe for cello (include bowings). Use bass clef and tenor clef only.

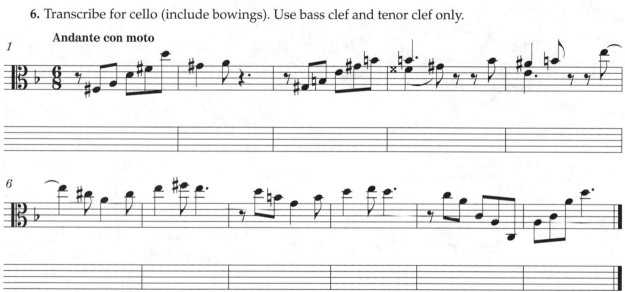

7. Transcribe for violin (include bowings).

8. Transcribe for cello using only tenor clef (include bowings).

9. There are errors in both of the transcriptions given below. Find them, circle them, and rewrite them on the blank staff.

a.

b.

Worksheet 2

Bowing

1. Bow all the string parts carefully in both of these excerpts from Handel's *Water Music*, Suite No. 1 in F major. You may benefit from listening to recordings of these two movements before you do the actual bowings.

Handel, *Water Music*, Suite No. 1 in F major

Overture, mm. 1–12

4. Supply two different bowings for this passage.

5. Listen to the following complete violin passage, played *non legato*. Then, for each of the twenty different bowings of the passage that you hear, write the letter corresponding to its correct notation.

Allegro moderato

0:25	**1.** _____	2:32	**6.** _____	5:07	**11.** _____	7:12	**16.** _____
0:48	**2.** _____	3:07	**7.** _____	5:33	**12.** _____	7:29	**17.** _____
1:17	**3.** _____	3:47	**8.** _____	6:00	**13.** _____	8:01	**18.** _____
1:42	**4.** _____	4:17	**9.** _____	6:25	**14.** _____	8:22	**19.** _____
2:07	**5.** _____	4:42	**10.** _____	6:50	**15.** _____	9:03	**20.** _____

Worksheet 3

String Harmonics

1. Write the notes that actually sound in this violin passage.

2. Write out the notes that actually sound in this cello passage.

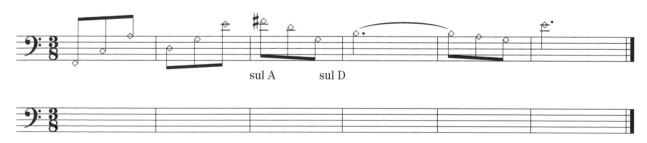

sul A   sul D

2. Study this canon by William Boyce and write it out on a separate sheet of manuscript paper as it would be realized by three singing voices. Canonic entrances are indicated by the numbers (1., 2., 3.) above the staff. Then complete the version for string orchestra, most of which is given below.

- Notice that parts have been added to this realization; you don't have to follow the original canon scheme entirely.

- Try to maintain an eighteenth-century style.

Boyce, "Epitaph"

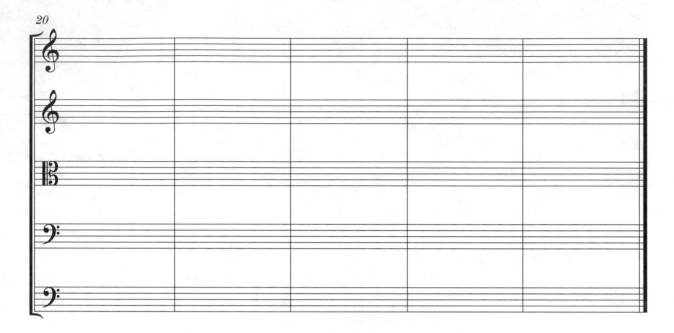

3. On a separate sheet of manuscript paper, continue the arrangement of this canon by Luigi Cherubini in the same manner as we begin it below, making certain that the original melody is heard throughout in one of the voices.

- You may wish to keep the melody in the second violin part all the way through.

- Do keep some independent voice or voices going until the end.

- Notice some elaborations in handling the original tune, for instance, in the viola part (measures 2–3); you may certainly treat the tune freely throughout.

Cherubini, "Solmisation" (three-voice canon)

4. Here are four different harmonizations by Bach of the same chorale tune. Make a different string orchestra version for each of these harmonizations.

- You may transpose the harmonization, put the chorale tune into an inner voice, or vary the original in any other way, but do not change the harmony or the melody.

- Supply dynamics and bowings for each of your orchestrations.

Bach, Four Settings of a Chorale Tune

a.

b.

c.

d.

5. Transcribe this passage from Aaron Copland's *Piano Variations* for a large string orchestra.

- Watch the dynamics and see that they can be realized in your orchestration exactly as the composer had in mind.

- Do not add extra octaves where these are not called for in the excerpt.

- You may want to use some solo parts instead of having the entire section play certain lines.

Copland, *Piano Variations,* 10 – 12

6. Here are two canons by the composer Joseph Haydn.

- The canons have already been realized so that you can see how the harmony works when all four voices sound. Transcribe each canon for full string orchestra.

- If you wish to transpose one or both canons or wish to have octave transpositions any time, feel free to do that at any place as long as it makes musical sense.

- Supply your own dynamics as well as bowings.

Haydn, *Die zehn Gebote der Kunst,* **Canon No. II**

Original format realized for the first canon.

Haydn, *Die zehn Gebote der Kunst,* **Canon No. III**

Original format realized for the second canon.

Listen and Score 1

Haydn, Menuetto al Rovescio, mm. 1–10

- Listen to the excerpt with the piano reduction as many times as necessary. Then notate what you hear in full score.

- After you have finished, compare your realization to a full score.

Listen and Score 2

Haydn, Symphony No. 100 ("Military"), second movement, mm. 1–8

- Listen to the excerpt with the piano reduction as many times as necessary. Then notate what you hear in full score.

- After you have finished, compare your realization to a full score.

Listen and Score 3

Grieg, Piano Concerto, second movement, mm. 1–8

- Listen to the excerpt with the piano reduction as many times as necessary. Then notate what you hear in full score.

- After you have finished, compare your realization to a full score.

Listen and Score 4

Vivaldi, Concerto Grosso, Op. 11, No. 4, second movement, mm. 105–111

- Listen to the excerpt with the piano reduction as many times as necessary. Then notate what you hear in full score.

- After you have finished, compare your realization to a full score.

Listen and Score 5

Mozart, Divertimento, K. 247, Menuetto, mm. 1–12

- Listen to the excerpt with the piano reduction as many times as necessary. Then notate what you hear in full score.

- After you have finished, compare your realization to a full score.

Listen and Score 6

Schubert, *Rosamunde*, **Overture, mm. 1–8**

- Listen to the excerpt with the piano reduction as many times as necessary. Then notate what you hear in full score.

- After you have finished, compare your realization to a full score.

Listen and Score 7

Beethoven, Symphony No. 3 ("Eroica"), second movement, mm. 1–8

- Listen to the excerpt with the piano reduction as many times as necessary. Then notate what you hear in full score.

- After you have finished, compare your realization to a full score.

Listen and Score 8

Tchaikovsky, *Serenade for Strings*, **Waltz, mm. 1–21**

- Listen to the excerpt with the piano reduction as many times as necessary. Then notate what you hear in full score.

- After you have finished, compare your realization to a full score.

Listen and Score 9

Dvořák, Cello Concerto, second movement, mm. 1–9

- Listen to the excerpt with the piano reduction as many times as necessary. Then notate what you hear in full score.

- After you have finished, compare your realization to a full score.

Worksheet 5

Harp

1. Give letter and pictorial representations of the pedal settings for the following glissandi above each example. Add enharmonic pitches to each example to make a smooth glissando possible. (See example a.)

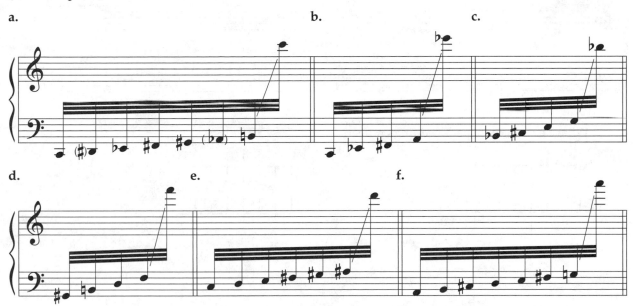

a.   **b.**   **c.**

d.   **e.**   **f.**

2. Arrange the following two passages so that they can be played on the harp. Use enharmonic spellings to make the pedaling possible. You may need to omit, add, or rearrange notes to make the chords more effective in the harp version.

Piano Version   **Harp Version**

String Version

Harp Version

3. What keys do these pedal settings reflect?

a.

b.

c.

d.

Worksheet 6

Transcribing for String Orchestra and Harp

1. Score this excerpt from Schubert's famous "Trout" Quintet for string orchestra and harp.

- There are obvious passages where the harp can be used, but these may not be the only ones in which you may want to use it. You might double the harp passages, though this may not always be appropriate.

- Some of your decisions may be influenced by the dynamics given in the score.

Schubert, Piano Quintet ("Trout"), Op. 114, first movement, mm. 1–26

2. Score this piece for string orchestra and harp.

- Retain the texture but make it as orchestrally colorful as possible.

- Use your ingenuity in handling the bass tremolos. You may add octaves up or down, but keep the tremolos very soft.

Liszt, "Nuages gris"

3. Transcribe this Bartók piano piece called "Slightly Tipsy" for string orchestra and harp.

- You may want to think of orchestrating this excerpt so that phrases form contrasting moods.
- Feel free to use octave transpositions.
- Again, watch the dynamics and orchestrate these with special instruments.

Bartók, "Slightly Tipsy," from *Three Burlesques*, mm. 11–28

4. Transcribe this Ravel piano piece for string orchestra and harp.

- Most of this orchestration should be quite obvious, but be sure the string orchestra is scored so that it sounds quite lush.

- Also be careful that the intended melodic line comes through well.

Ravel, "Une barque sur l'océan," from Miroirs, mm. 33–40

Test Yourself II

Woodwinds

1. Name the four woodwind families. _____

_____

2. What does the word *embouchure* mean? _____

_____

3. What is meant by overblowing? _____

_____

4. If the sounding pitch is middle C (C⁴), what is the written pitch for the following instruments?

    a. alto clarinet _____

    b. soprano saxophone _____

    c. D clarinet (piccolo) _____

    d. E♭ clarinet _____

    e. C clarinet _____

    f. tenor saxophone _____

    g. B♭ clarinet _____

    h. English horn _____

    i. alto flute _____

    j. alto saxophone _____

5. If the written pitch is middle C (C⁴), what is the sounding pitch for the following instruments?

    a. alto clarinet _____

    b. soprano saxophone _____

    c. D clarinet (piccolo) _____

    d. E♭ clarinet (piccolo) _____

    e. C clarinet _____

    f. tenor saxophone _____

    g. B♭ clarinet _____

    h. English horn _____

    i. alto flute _____

    j. alto saxophone _____

6. What does a slur mean to a wind player? _____

_____

7. Name four ways the player produces vibrato on a woodwind instrument. _____

_____

8. How does one designate a passage to be played without vibrato? _____

_____

9. How is double and triple tonguing achieved on woodwind instruments? _____

_____

10. Describe flutter tonguing. What is the German word for it? _____

_____

11. If two oboes are to play the same part, what is the marking on the score? _____

12. How does one designate the second clarinet to play a passage alone if first and second are notated on the same line? _____

13. Why is the designation *solo* sometimes used? Why is it superfluous? _____

_____

_____

_____

_____

_____

14. What are multiphonics? _____

_____

_____

15. Name some special effects for woodwinds in use today. _____

_____

_____

_____

16. Give the written ranges of the following instruments:

a. piccolo   **c.** alto flute   **e.** oboe

b. flute   **d.** bass flute   **f.** English horn

g. all clarinets' written range   **i.** bassoon   **k.** oboe d'amore

h. all saxophones' written range   **j.** contrabassoon

    17. Name the first three registers of the clarinet. _____

_____

    18. What are the registral characteristics of the following instruments?

        a. flute: _____

        b. oboe: _____

        c. English horn: _____

        d. bassoon _____

    19. What is meant by the *break* on the clarinet? _____

_____

_____

    20. What can an orchestrator not expect from woodwinds that may be routinely expected from strings? _____

_____

_____

Worksheet 7

Woodwind Transposition

1. Supply the transposition requested in each of the exercises below.

j.

2. Mark an **x** over, under, or next to all pitch errors in transposition, incorrect accidentals, and outright wrong notes in the two arrangements given below.

Chopin, Nocturne, Op. 37, No. 1, mm. 1–7

Beethoven, Piano Sonata, Op. 27, No. 2 ("Moonlight"), second movement, mm. 8–16

Worksheet 8

Transcribing for Woodwinds in Pairs

   1. Transcribe this excerpt of Andrew Imbrie's Serenade for flute, viola, and piano for woodwinds in pairs.

- Use your imagination to utilize this combination in the most effective way to bring out the solo voices as well as what would be "accompaniment."

- You may want to "thicken" some one-line voices, but be careful to keep the harmonic style.

Imbrie, Serenade, third movement

2. Transcribe this most unusual *Menuetto al Rovescio* for woodwinds in pairs.

- You may want to use octave transpositions, and also double any parts to make it more effective for this woodwind combination.

- You might consider emphasizing the unique nature of this piece—the retrograde of the first line of music by the second line—by means of the orchestration.

Haydn, Menuetto al Rovescio and Trio, mm. 1–44

Worksheet 9

Transcribing for Woodwinds and Strings

1. Transcribe this excerpt from Dvořák's Piano Quintet for woodwinds in pairs and string orchestra.

- Feel free to double pairs or add octaves where appropriate.
- Emphasize the melodic lines carefully, and take care to observe the dynamics throughout.

Dvořák, Piano Quintet, Op. 81, second movement, mm. 128–144

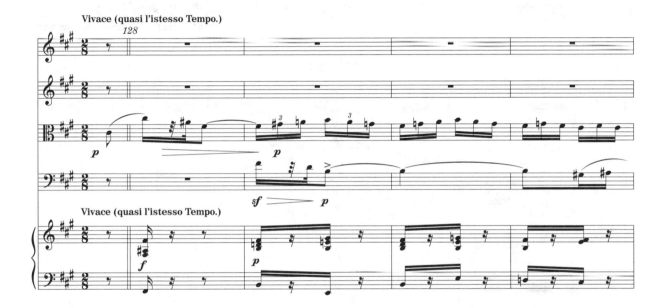

2. This excerpt from Schumann's Piano Quartet lends itself well for scoring. Score this for woodwinds in pairs and string orchestra.

- Make certain to keep the light, magical flavor of the piece. You may opt to have only one section on even one instrument where Schumann has octave doublings.

- At other places you may want to have octave transpositions as well as emphasizing some pitches to bring out the rhythm.

Schumann, Piano Quartet, Op. 47, Scherzo, mm. 1–52

3. This piano piece by Gottfried von Einem is to be orchestrated for woodwinds in pairs and string orchestra.

- You may want to thicken the texture at various points, but study the harmony closely so that any added pitches fit the style.

- Keep the overall feeling light and bright throughout.

Einem, Klavierstück, mm. 1–22

4. The Martinů Quintet excerpt is also to be transcribed for pairs of winds and string orchestra.

- Octave transpositions are suggested throughout, as well as an emphasis of the canonic nature of the piece.
- Forget about the pizzicato suggested in the score and make your own orchestral decisions.
- Again, added pitches are allowed as long as they make harmonic sense in the style.

Martinů, String Quintet, third movement, mm. 1–34

5. Transcribe the piano part of this Schubert song for pairs of winds, string orchestra, and harp.

- Notice that Schubert doubles the voice part all the time. Use your imagination in the "coloring" of that line.

- Keep the orchestration transparent so that the voice can be heard at all times.

Schubert, "Der Pilgrim," mm. 1–38

Pil - ger - sta - be zog ich fort mit Kindersinn. Denn mich trieb ein

mäch - tig Hof - fen und ein dunk - les Glau - bens - wort, wand - le, rief's, der Weg ist of - fen,

im - mer nach dem Aufgang fort.

Worksheet 10

Transcribing for a Large Orchestral Woodwind Section

1. Transcribe this Schoenberg piano piece for a large wind section.

- You may add octaves but no new pitches.

- This gives many chances for odd but interesting combinations of instruments.

- Suggested instrumentation: piccolo, 2 flutes, 2 oboes, English horn, 2 clarinets, bass clarinet, 2 bassoons, and contrabassoon.

- Remember: Even if an instrument plays only two or three pitches that is fine in such a short piece.

Schoenberg, Kleines Klavierstück, Op. 19, No. 2

2. Orchestrate this Debussy prelude for a large woodwind section, strings, and harp.

- Vary the color of the tune in as many ways as possible, but always in good taste!

- Use the harp sparingly so that its appearance is meaningful.

- Use the auxiliary wind instruments (English horn, bass clarinet, contrabassoon, etc.) to good advantage.

- Fill out chords at will, using octave doublings.

Debussy, Preludes, Book I, "La Fille aux cheveux de lin," mm. 1–19

Listen and Score 10

Mozart, Divertimento in B♭, K. 270, second movement, mm. 1–8

- Listen to the excerpt with the piano reduction as many times as necessary. Then notate what you hear in full score.

- After you have finished, compare your realization to a full score.

Listen and Score 11

Mozart, Divertimento in B♭, K. 270, third movement, mm. 1–8

- Listen to the excerpt with the piano reduction as many times as necessary. Then notate what you hear in full score.

- After you have finished, compare your realization to a full score.

Listen and Score 12

Mozart, Symphony No. 40, K. 550, third movement, mm. 1–20

- Listen to the excerpt with the piano reduction as many times as necessary. Then notate what you hear in full score.

- After you have finished, compare your realization to a full score.

Listen and Score 13

Brahms, Serenade in A major, Op. 16, first movement, mm. 1–9

- Listen to the excerpt with the piano reduction as many times as necessary. Then notate what you hear in full score.

- After you have finished, compare your realization to a full score.

Listen and Score 14

Mendelssohn, Symphony No. 3, fourth movement, mm. 1–10

- Listen to the excerpt with the piano reduction as many times as necessary. Then notate what you hear in full score.

- After you have finished, compare your realization to a full score.

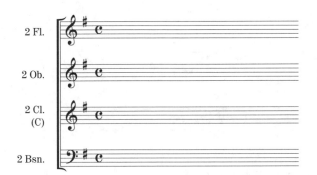

Listen and Score 15

Gounod, Petite Symphonie, first movement, mm. 16–26

- Listen to the excerpt with the piano reduction as many times as necessary. Then notate what you hear in full score.

- After you have finished, compare your realization to a full score.

Listen and Score 16

Tchaikovsky, *The Nutcracker* ballet, Overture, mm. 1–8

- Listen to the excerpt with the piano reduction as many times as necessary. Then notate what you hear in full score.

- After you have finished, compare your realization to a full score.

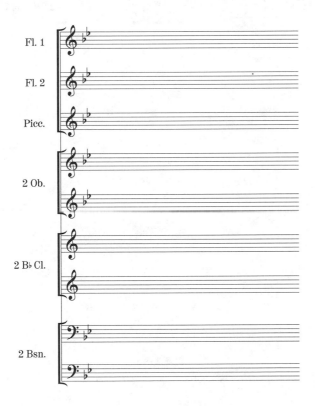

Listen and Score 17

Tchaikovsky, "Capriccio Italien," Op. 45, mm. 1–15

- Listen to the excerpt with the piano reduction as many times as necessary. Then notate what you hear in full score.

- After you have finished, compare your realization to a full score.

Listen and Score 18

Wilbye, "Adieu, Sweet Amaryllis," mm. 1–7

- Listen to the excerpt with the piano reduction as many times as necessary. Then notate what you hear in full score.

- After you have finished, compare your realization to a full score.

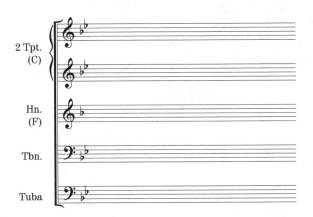

Test Yourself III

Brass

1. Describe the difference between a natural horn or trumpet and a valve horn or trumpet. _____

_____

_____

2. Notate the first seven partials of the harmonic series on F, E♭, B♭, and D.

a. on F

_____

b. on E♭

_____

c. on B♭

_____

d. on D

_____

3. Describe the differences between the trumpet, horn, trombone, and tuba mouthpieces. _____

_____

_____

_____

4. What was the highest partial demanded during the Classical period? _____

5. What is *clarino* playing? _____

_____

_____

6. What is a crook? How does it work? _____

_____

7. What is the difference in the transposition of the F horn and F trumpet? _____

_____

8. What does a valve do on a brass instrument? _____
_____
_____

9. Describe what happens when a trumpet player depresses:

    a. the first valve _____

    b. the second valve _____

    c. the third valve _____

    d. the first and third valve _____

    e. the second and third valve _____

    f. the first and second valve _____

    g. all three valves _____

10. What are the positions on the trombone? What effect do they have? _____
_____
_____
_____

11. How many positions are there on the tenor trombone? _____

12. Name the fundamental pitches in all positions on the tenor trombone. _____
_____

13. What are the positions on the bass trombone? _____
_____

14. What note is difficult to perform on the bass trombone unless a G♭ or E trigger is present?
_____

15. What does a mute do to a brass instrument? _____
_____

16. Which is the standard orchestral brass mute? _____

17. Name some other brass mutes. _____
_____
_____

18. What is a Wagner tuba? Name some composers other than Wagner who have used it.
_____
_____
_____

19. What is the major difference between a euphonium and a baritone? _____
_____

20. Name the usual brass complement of a large, modern symphony orchestra. _____

_____

_____

21. What do the designations "B♭ alto horn" and "B♭ basso horn" mean? What is the transposition of each? _____

_____

_____

22. If the sounding pitch is midde C (C⁴), what is the written pitch for a trumpet

    a. in B♭? _____   **c.** in D? _____

    b. in C? _____   **d.** in F? _____

23. What is the lowest written pitch for all trumpets? _____

24. Which of the following trills should be avoided on the trumpet?

25. Describe an ophicleide and its sound. _____

_____

_____

26. What is the range of the tuba?

_____

27. What do the pitch designations for the following tubas mean: F, B♭, E♭, C, or BB♭ tubas? Do these instruments transpose? _____

_____

28. How does the diameter of the bell contribute to the sound of the brass instrument?

_____

_____

29. How are horn trills produced? _____

_____

Worksheet 11

Brass Transposition

Supply the transposition requested in each of the exercises below.

e.

f.

g. Similar to Mahler, Symphony No. 3, first movement, one measure before 7.

h.

i.

j.

Worksheet 12

Transcribing for Woodwinds in Pairs and Horns

1. Transcribe this Max Reger "Humoresque" for pairs of winds and two horns in F.

- You may certainly use octave transpositions.
- Give the horns a significant part to play in the piece.
- Use ideas of "background–foreground" scoring.

Max Reger, "Humoresque," Op. 20, No. 2, mm. 1–18

2. Orchestrate this Mendelssohn "Song without Words" for pairs of winds and four horns.

- Again, you will probably want to add octaves at places.
- Color each phrase a bit differently; you have enough instruments to do so.

Mendelssohn, Song without Words, Op. 53, No. 5, "Volkslied," mm. 1–35

3. Score this excerpt from a Brahms String Quintet for woodwinds in pairs and four horns

- Once again, octave transpositions may be advisable.
- Follow the dynamics closely and if you wish to thicken the texture, be careful that the harmony remains stylistically correct.

Brahms, String Quintet, Op. 111, fourth movement, mm. 1–38

Worksheet 13

Transcribing for Brass

1. Complete the arrangement of Schubert's canon below in the manner in which it is begun. Be sure to supply all accidentals. Then, on a separate sheet of manuscript paper, make a second version of it using the same ensemble but orchestrating it quite differently.

Schubert, "Der Schnee zerrinnt"

2. Transcribe this interlude from Hindemith's *Ludus Tonalis* for a large brass section: 4, 3, 3, 1.

- You may need to worry about ranges from measures 15 on, but if you use trumpets in C, the D♭ is more easily playable. Alternatively, you may decide to use a lower octave.

- Do not be fooled by the piano scoring at the beginning. These are simply changing notes, and both right and left hand can be played by the same group of instruments.

- See that from measure 19 on the instrumentation mirrors the change in the mood of the piece.

Hindemith, "Interludium," from *Ludus Tonalis*, mm. 1–27

Listen and Score 19

Dvořák, Symphony No. 9 ("From the New World"), second movement, mm. 1–5

- Listen to the excerpt with the piano reduction as many times as necessary. Then notate what you hear in full score.

- After you have finished, compare your realization to a full score.

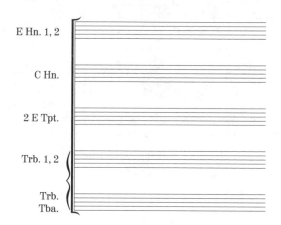

Listen and Score 20

Mussorgsky, Ravel, *Pictures at an Exhibition*, "Promenade," mm. 1–8

- Listen to the excerpt with the piano reduction as many times as necessary. Then notate what you hear in full score.

- After you have finished, compare your realization to a full score.

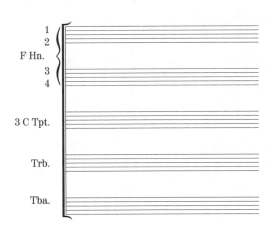

Listen and Score 21

Berlioz, *Symphonie fantastique*, fifth movement, mm. 207–216

- Listen to the excerpt with the piano reduction as many times as necessary. Then notate what you hear in full score.

- After you have finished, compare your realization to a full score.

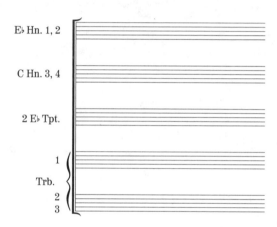

Listen and Score 22

- Listen to the excerpt with the piano reduction as many times as necessary. Then notate what you hear in full score.
- After you have finished, compare your realization to a full score.

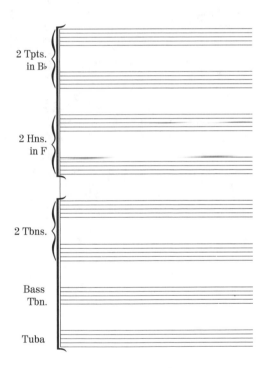

Listen and Score 23

Bartók, *Concerto for Orchestra*, second movement, mm. 123–156

- Listen to the excerpt with the piano reduction as many times as necessary. Then notate what you hear in full score.

- After you have finished, compare your realization to a full score.

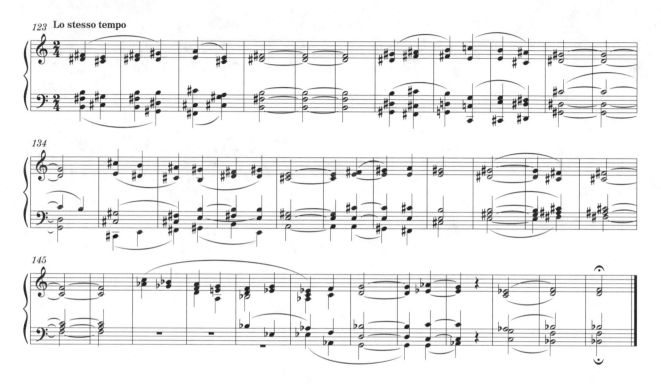

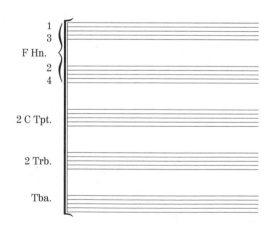

Worksheet 14

Transcribing for a Large Orchestral Brass Section

1. Transcribe the beginning of the last movement of Brahms's Horn Trio for large orchestral brass section.

- The solo horn part need not be performed by a solo horn.

- You surely have to use a great deal of octave transposition.

- If a thicker harmony is suggested by the music, you should flesh out the score, keeping in mind the light touch of the piece.

Brahms, Horn Trio, Op. 40, fourth movement, mm. 1–31

2. Transcribe this excerpt for a large brass section.

- Supply your own dynamics and instrumental spacing, allowing the music to guide your choices.

Stirling, *Romantic Pieces for the Organ,* "Maestoso," mm. 1–26

3. Transcribe this piece for a large orchestral brass section.

- Be sure to keep the melody legato.

- Try to build effective dynamic changes.

- You may thicken the harmony and strengthen the melody with doublings, but do not alter the character of the piece.

Kabalevsky, "Toccatina," mm. 1–49

Worksheet 15

Transcribing for Woodwinds and Brass

Orchestrate this portion of the Chopin Piano Sonata in B♭ Minor for large orchestral brass section and woodwind section.

- Because of the piano range you will have to adjust the octave transpositions. However, do it for an entire phrase, not abruptly in the middle of a phrase.

- Be creative in scoring the left-hand arpeggios. There needs to be a great deal of interlocking for smoothness.

- Also notice the use of the sustaining pedal. This should give you a hint of possible sustained chords with the moving eighth notes.

Chopin, Sonata for Piano, Op. 35, first movement, mm. 169–214

Listen and Score 24

Beethoven, Symphony No. 8, second movement, mm. 1–7

- Listen to the excerpt with the piano reduction as many times as necessary. Then notate what you hear in full score.

- After you have finished, compare your realization to a full score.

Listen and Score 25

Mozart, Symphony No. 40 (K. 550), third movement, mm. 7–14

- Listen to the excerpt with the piano reduction as many times as necessary. Then notate what you hear in full score.

- After you have finished, compare your realization to a full score.

Listen and Score 26

Weber, *Euryanthe*, Overture, mm. 13–25

- Listen to the excerpt with the piano reduction as many times as necessary. Then notate what you hear in full score.

- After you have finished, compare your realization to a full score.

Test Yourself IV

1. Define the following terms as they apply to percussion instruments, and then name some percussion instruments in each category.

a. idiophones _____

_____

_____

b. membranophones _____

_____

c. aerophones _____

_____

_____

2. Explain the difference between percussion instruments of definite pitch and those of indefinite pitch. _____

_____

_____

3. What are the various ways to notate percussion instruments? _____

_____

_____

4. What other factors must be taken into account when notating a percussion section in a score? _____

_____

_____

5. Give the percussion layout for the following instruments in a full orchestral score: triangle, xylophone, güiro, glockenspiel, timpani, snare drum, marimba, bass drum.

_____

_____

6. Give the ranges of the following instruments:

a. marimba   **b.** vibraphone   **c.** crotales

d. xylophone

e. glockenspiel

f. chimes

g. timpani

h. roto toms

7. Notate the following effects:

    a. four-stroke ruff _____

    b. flam _____

    c. drag _____

    d. roll _____

8. Notate a roll on cymbals or membranophones two different ways.

9. What is the main difference between finger cymbals and crotales? _____

_____

10. What is a slapstick or whip? _____

_____

11. How does one tune timpani? What sizes do they usually come in? _____

_____

_____

12. What are the similarities and differences between tom-toms and timbales? How many of each can

one use? _____

_____

_____

_____

13. What kind of sticks, mallets, or beaters are used for the following instruments:

    a. triangle _____

    b. tom-tom _____

    c. cymbals _____

    d. conga drum _____

    e. crotales _____

14. Describe the cimbalom used in a modern symphony orchestra. _____

_____

15. Give the range of the organ pedals.

_____

16. Give the ranges of the harpsichord and celesta.

   a. harpsichord   **b.** celesta

17. How has the piano been used as a percussion instrument in the last hundred years?

_____

_____

18. Name all the transposing percussion and keyboard instruments and state how they

transpose. _____

_____

19. What is a prepared piano? _____

_____

Worksheet 16

Transcribing for Non-Pitched Percussion

1. Transcribe the following excerpt for non-pitched percussion.

- Use four percussionists playing a variety of instruments. For instance:

    Player 1 — 5 or 6 temple blocks.

    Player 2 — 2 bongos plus 3 or 4 tom-toms.

    Player 3 — 2 timbales, 3 wood blocks, and a bass or conga drum.

    Player 4 — suspended cymbals and triangles.

- The sustained pedal should be kept as such, but you may color it quite imaginatively.

- Using too many instruments per theme will distort the effect of that theme's statement.

Bach, Toccata and Fugue (BWV 540), mm. 1–82

118

2. Transcribe for non-pitched percussion using four players. Use instruments similar to those employed for the previous exercise, but in different combinations.

Bach, Prelude and Fugue (BWV 541), mm. 1–38

120

Worksheet 17

Transcribing for Pitched and Non-Pitched Percussion

1. Transcribe for four percussionists.

- Color the "stamp" in various ways, using both non-pitched and pitched instruments; involve the marimba, xylophone, and vibraphone, but never use a simple stamp of the foot.

Joplin, "Stoptime Rag," mm. 1–19

2. Transcribe this piano piece by Godziatski for pitched and nonpitched percussion instruments using four performers.

Godziatski, "Surface Scratches," mm. 1–26

3. Transcribe this piece for two players using a variety of pitched and non-pitched instruments.

- If necessary, both players should be capable of playing two instruments at the same time in certain places.

Riegger, "Tone Clusters," mm. 1–30

Worksheet 18

Two Transcriptions by Tchaikovsky

Tchaikovsky transcribed two short dances by Mozart, one called Minuet and the other Gigue, and he included them in his Fourth Orchestral Suite titled "Mozartiana." Study Tchaikovsky's transcriptions, each of which is preceded by the original piano piece. Pay particular attention to the skillful and tasteful way in which Tchaikovsky orchestrated these pieces without compromising Mozart's style. Notice also the stylistic orchestral treatment Tchaikovsky gives to both excerpts, particularly his treatment of measures 7–11 in the Gigue.

After studying these pieces, listen to recordings of them, and look also at the piano pieces by Tchaikovsky that Stravinsky orchestrated for *The Fairy's Kiss*. Stravinsky does a masterful job in his transcription, greatly enhancing the music yet keeping the spirit of Tchaikovsky's music intact.

Minuet

Mozart, Menuetto (K. 355/576b), mm. 1–23

Tchaikovsky, Suite No. 4 ("Mozartiana"), Menuet, mm. 1–23

Gigue

Mozart, Gigue (K. 574), mm. 1–16

Worksheet 19

Transcribing for Woodwinds in Pairs, Percussion, and Strings

Score this tango for woodwinds in pairs, two percussion players, and strings.

- Use some non-Western percussion instruments, but do it with good taste.
- You may use octave transpositions, but do not add notes to the already rich harmonies.
- Try to keep Stravinsky's typically lean sound.

Stravinsky, "Tango," mm. 1–24

Worksheet 20

Transcribing for Woodwinds in Threes, Brass, and Percussion

Orchestrate the opening of the last movement of Mendelssohn's famous String Octet for winds in threes, a small brass section (2, 2, 2, 1), timpani, and two percussionists.

- There are many chances here for effective octave doublings.

- Always keep the light quality of the music except in obvious tutti places.

- Since Mendelssohn never used more than a few percussion instruments, your use may not be stylistically "correct," but for this exercise don't worry about it.

Mendelssohn, String Octet, Op. 20, fourth movement, mm. 1–51

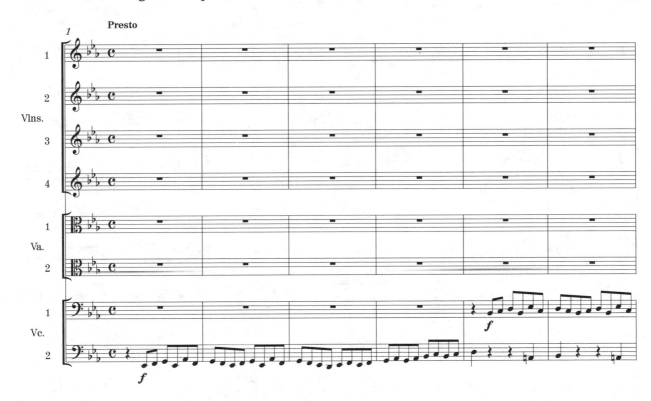

Worksheet 21

Transcribing for Woodwinds in Pairs, Harp, Strings, and Percussion

Orchestrate this Ravel piano piece for pairs of woodwinds, harp, strings, and two percussionists.

- Octave doublings are allowed.

- Color these impressionistic gestures richly.

- Be very imaginative in orchestrating the ostinato, changing color often.

Ravel, "La Vallée des cloches," from *Miroirs*, mm. 1–16

Worksheet 22

Reducing a Full Orchestral Score to a Piano Score

Before transcribing piano or vocal works for full orchestra, it is beneficial to become adept at identifying the essential elements of a full orchestral score by reducing that score to a piano score. The orchestrator must be able to isolate the main melodic and harmonic lines from doublings that simply add color and power. This skill will enable him or her to create a piano score of a large vocal or choral work to be used by an accompanist, or a condensed piano score of a concerto or other symphonic work. In addition, it makes the task of orchestrating a piano score much easier to handle.

Here are a few things to keep in mind when creating reduced scores:

- It is not necessary to double notes that are doubled in the full score. Decide on the best sounding octave and stick to it unless the entire piece shifts up or down in range. Try to make your reduction playable by one pianist.

- If the score is so complex that more than two lines are needed for the piano realization, use three or even more staves, as long as one pianist is able to perform your reduction. Many piano pieces composed during the last one hundred years use more than two staves.

- Take note of all transpositions in the full score—for instance, the four horns or the horns and trumpets may be in two different keys. Also, remember that in Mozart, Rossini, and even Beethoven scores the two timpani are notated with C for tonic and G for dominant, no matter the actual key of the piece. The thinking behind this practice was that the timpani "take on" the bass pitches of the orchestra. However, you should write the correct pitches in your reduction.

We provide the first few measures for each of the five reduction exercises; copy these measures onto separate manuscript paper before you continue the reductions on your own.

1. Mozart, *Don Giovanni*, **Overture, mm. 1–21**

Andante

2. Rossini, *The Barber of Seville*, Overture, mm. 1–17

Andante maestoso

3. Beethoven, *The Creatures of Prometheus,* Overture, mm. 1–15

152

4. Wagner, *Tannhäuser*, Overture, mm. 142–157

154

Tempo I

5. Verdi, *Falstaff*, Act II, Scene 1, end, at [25]

Worksheet 23

Transcribing for Classical Orchestra

Transcribe the theme from Mozart's Variations in G on a theme by Salieri for Classical orchestra.

- You may thicken the texture by adding the appropriate pitches alluded to in the harmony, even in the solo voices.

- Doublings are of course allowed.

Mozart, Variations in G, K. 180, Variation 6, mm. 1–16

Minuetto. Andante

Worksheet 24

Transcribing for a Beethoven Orchestra

Transcribe this excerpt from Beethoven's *Diabelli Variations* for an orchestra used in early Beethoven works: winds in pairs, 2 horns, 2 trumpets, timpani, and strings. This is a tempestuous passage. You may wish to listen to some Beethoven symphonies, perhaps the first and fourth movements of the third symphony, in which you will find typical Beethoven treatment of the *sf*.

- Notice the octaves in the second part of the variation; give them special and colorful orchestrations.

Beethoven, *Diabelli Variations*, **Op. 120, Variation 28, mm. 1–32**

Worksheet 25

Transcribing for a Small Romantic Orchestra

Orchestrate this fugato from Mendelssohn's String Quintet No. 1 for small Romantic orchestra: 2, 2, 2; 2, 2; timpani and strings.

- Octave doublings are certainly allowed, but they should not be used all the time.

- Again you may thicken the texture in spots, but use only pitches that fit into the implied harmony.

Mendelssohn, Quintet, Op. 18, third movement, mm. 1–54

Worksheet 26

Transcribing for Full Orchestra

1. Orchestrate these two Webern Bagatelles for full modern orchestra.

- Keep the pointillistic nature of the pieces alive without much, if any, doubling.

- The dynamics are of the greatest importance here, and if there are a great number of rests for many instruments, that is the nature of this music.

- It is suggested that you listen to the Webern Symphony before doing this assignment.

Webern, Two Bagatelles

Ziemlich fließend ($\quad$ = ca 76)

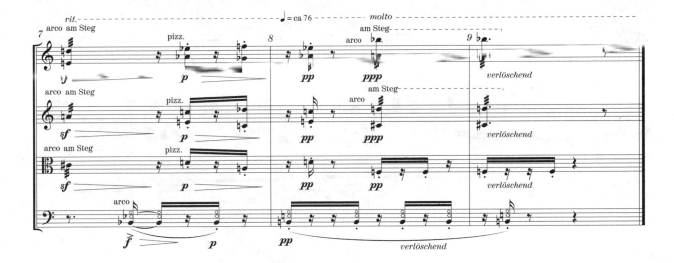

2. Transcribe this chorale prelude for full orchestra.

- Be creative in how you color the chorale tune.

- You need not confine the contrapuntal lines to their given registers.

- Observe the dynamic markings in your transcription.

Smyth, "Du, O schönes Weltgebäude!" mm. 1–7

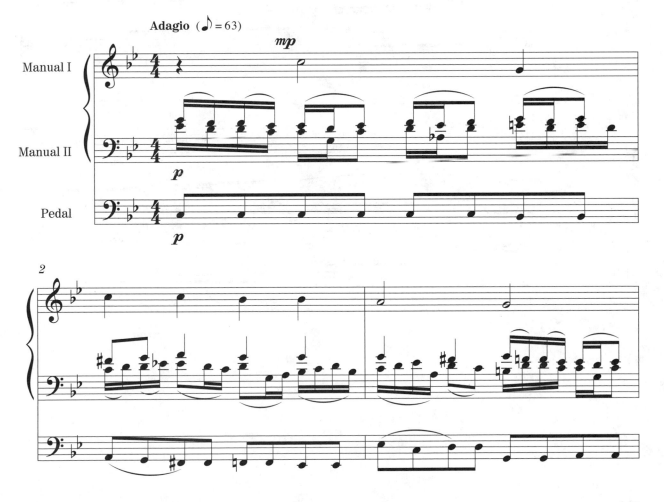

3. Orchestrate this piece for full orchestra with at least two percussionists.

- It is strongly suggested that you organize the piece with bar lines—otherwise it would be too difficult to conduct and keep the orchestra together.

- When there is a long passage of repeated notes, sustained chords made up of these repeated pitches may be quite effective.

- Reserve some great power for the passages marked *fff*. Here is an opportunity to use the full orchestra with many octave extensions downward.

Karamanov, "Epilog"

4. Score this excerpt from "New Rag" by Scott Joplin for full orchestra.

- You may or may not want to score the repeat of the first section differently from the first time.
- Keep the "dancey" flavor of the piece and watch the dynamics for changes of color.

Joplin, "New Rag," mm. 1–36

Worksheet 27

Transcribing for a Large Impressionistic Orchestra

    1. Transcribe this Debussy piano prelude for a large Impressionistic orchestra.

- It is strongly suggested that you listen to Debussy's "La Mer" before attempting this orchestration.

- Notice the great subtleness of the dynamics and tailor your orchestration accordingly

- There is an ostinato in measure 18. Use your imagination in coloring it in various ways to make it very interesting, without obscuring the melody.

Debussy, "Les Sons et les parfums tournent dans l'air du soir," from *Preludes for the Piano*, mm. 1–30

2. Ravel orchestrated many of his own piano pieces, including *Valses nobles et sentimentales* and *Le Tombeau de Couperin.* He did not orchestrate his *Sonatine,* but it lends itself well to that treatment.

- You might wish to study some of Ravel's great orchestral works, such as *La Valse* and his *Daphnis et Chloé, Suite No. 2,* before orchestrating this excerpt.

- The clear melody-accompaniment texture should lead you to treat this piece quite differently from the Debussy prelude.

Ravel, *Sonatine,* first movement, mm. 1–28

Listen and Score 27

Beethoven, *Egmont*, Overture, mm. 1–15

- Listen to the excerpt with the piano reduction as many times as necessary. Then notate what you hear in full score.

- After you have finished, compare your realization to a full score.

Listen and Score 28

Schubert, Symphony No. 8 ("Unfinished"), second movement, mm. 1–19

- Listen to the excerpt with the piano reduction as many times as necessary. Then notate what you hear in full score.

- After you have finished, compare your realization to a full score.

Listen and Score 29

- Listen to the excerpt with the piano reduction as many times as necessary. Then notate what you hear in full score.

- After you have finished, compare your realization to a full score.

Listen and Score 30

Rossini, *La Gazza ladra*, Overture, mm. 4–13

- Listen to the excerpt with the piano reduction as many times as necessary. Then notate what you hear in full score.

- After you have finished, compare your realization to a full score.

Worksheet 28

Transcribing for an Orchestra of Any Size

Transcribe this Brahms sextet passage for an orchestra you feel appropriate for this piece. A Romantic orchestra size is suggested.

● The harmony is so rich here that very few "new" pitches need to be added. Nevertheless, you may want to add octaves, and certainly double some passages.

Brahms, Sextet, Op. 18, third movement (Scherzo), mm. 1–42

Worksheet 29

Transcribing for Clarinet and Small Orchestra

Orchestrate this excerpt from Beethoven's Quintet for piano, oboe, clarinet, horn, and bassoon for clarinet and small orchestra.

- It may be wise to bring in the soloists at measure 37 and have a rather long orchestral prelude.

- Of course, octave doublings in important orchestral gestures are encouraged.

Beethoven, Piano Quintet, Op. 16, first movement, mm. 22–52

Worksheet 30

Transcribing for Harp and Strings

Here is a piano piece by the American composer Joseph Schwantner, which is to be orchestrated for harp and string orchestra.

- Practice your harp pedal settings by giving them in the harp part.

- If enharmonic notations are necessary, give them correctly in your score.

Schwantner, *Veiled Autumn,* **mm. 1–25**

Worksheet 31

Transcribing for Flute, Two Oboes, and String Orchestra

Transcribe the viola part into an effective flute register.

- You might wish to change the key of the piece in your transcription.

- Do not change the basic harmony, but don't feel obligated to adhere to the register of the piano realization.

Vivaldi, "Giga," mm. 1–13

Worksheet 32

Transcribing for Voice and String Orchestra

Transcribe these two Bach chorales, the first for soprano and strings, the second for tenor and strings.

- Keeping the basic harmony intact, try to invent figuration that will sound like accompaniment.

- You may transpose either chorale to a different key if necessary, but do not change the tune for any reason.

Bach, "Ein' feste Burg ist unser Gott"

Bach, "Ich dank' dir, lieber Herre"

Worksheet 33

Transcribing Vocal Accompaniments: Small Orchestra

1. Transcribe this Mozart song so that the voice is accompanied by flute and strings.

● In the original, the voice is not exactly (rhythmically) doubled until measure 4; you may want to do the same in your transcription.

● You may flesh out the string accompaniment and you many want to compose a new obbligato part for the solo flute; however, stay in the style of Mozart.

Mozart, "Der Zauberer" ("The Magician")

wie,? ich seuf - zte, zit - ter - te, und schien mich doch zu freu'n; glaubt mir, er
pfand? ich sah, ich hör - te nichts, sprach nichts als Ja und Nein; glaubt mir, er
her; was würd', o Göt - ter, sonst nach so viel Zau - be - rei'n, aus mir zu-

muss ein Zaub' - rer sein.
muss ein Zaub' - rer sein.
muss ein Zaub' - rer sein.
letzt ge - wor - den sein!

2. Transcribe the accompaniment of this Wolf song for pairs of woodwinds, two horns, harp, and strings.

- The harmony is very rich, with many doublings. While keeping all these pitches, see if you can make your orchestration very transparent so that the voice part will be heard well whenever it is present.

Wolf, "Reflections"

Ziemlich gemessen

Fei - ger Ge - dan - ken
Fears that e'er haunt us,

Worksheet 34

Transcribing Vocal Accompaniments: Medium-Sized Orchestra

Orchestrate this Charles Ives song for large orchestra and voice.

- Again, in this orchestration make certain that the singer can be heard, even when he or she is not in the most penetrating part of the voice.

- Since the accompaniment repeats, there is a great opportunity for color changes.

- Do not add octaves or unnecessary extra pitches. Doubling at pitch can be effective.

Ives, "The Last Reader," text by Oliver Wendell Holmes

They lie up-on my path-way bleak, Those flowers that once ran wild, As on a fa-ther's care-worn cheek The ring-lets of his child; The gold-en ming-ling with the gray, and steal-ing half its snows a-way.

Worksheet 35

Transcribing Vocal Accompaniments: Large Orchestra

Transcribe this excerpt for a large orchestra.

- Keep the sustained chords of the accompaniment in their given register, but use your imagination in coloring them.

R. Strauss, "Ruhe, meine Seele," Op. 27, No. 1, mm. 1–21

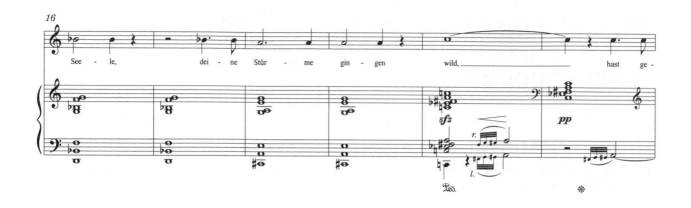

See - le,   dei - ne Stür - me gin - gen   wild, _____ hast ge -

Worksheet 36

Transcribing Vocal Accompaniments: Woodwinds, Two Horns, Harp, Percussion, and Strings

Transcribe this excerpt for woodwinds, two horns, harp, percussion, and strings.

● Score for as many percussion instruments (for one player) as you desire.

Debussy, *Trois mélodies*, "Le Son du cor s'afflige," mm. 1–23

bise er- rant en courts a- bois

L'â- me du loup pleu- re dans cet- te

voix

Qui monte a- vec le so- leil qui dé- cli- ne

D'une a- gonie__ on veut croire ca- li- ne

Et qui ra- vit et qui navre à la

fois.

Worksheet 37

Transcribing for Chorus, Brass, and Strings

Transcribe this excerpt for chorus, brass, and strings.

- You may want to double the chorus parts sometimes with brass and other times with strings.

- Since no dynamics are given, supply your own and let them be reflected in your orchestration.

Buxtehude, "Das neugeborne Kindelein," mm. 37–68

Worksheet 38

Transcribing Choral Accompaniments: Medium-Sized Orchestra

Transcribe this choral piece for chorus and medium-sized orchestra.

- You may add instrumental doublings, but do not change the harmony.

"Ye Watchers and Ye Holy Ones" (Gustav Holst's setting of the traditional Easter hymn)

Worksheet 39

Transcribing Choral Accompaniments: Medium-Sized Orchestra and Harp

Transcribe the choral accompaniment for medium-sized orchestra and harp.

● You may also wish to double the voice parts at times.

Schubert, "The Lord is My Shepherd," arr. by Sir John Stainer, mm. 1–21

215

Worksheet 40

Transcribing for Available Combinations of Instruments

Transcribe the following six excerpts for any combination of instruments available in your class. Consider the strengths and weaknesses of each performer and tailor your orchestration accordingly.

- If you use piano, try to create an independent part for it rather than a simple reduction of the score.
- Try to cover all the pitches in each excerpt even if you have to import a few performers.

1. Grieg, "Røtnams-Knut," Op. 72, No. 7, mm. 1–30

2. Previn, "February 15," from *Five Pages from My Calendar*, mm. 1–25

3. León, "Ritual," mm. 1–13

4. Haydn, Symphony No. 103 ("Drum Roll"), third movement, mm. 1–27

5. Beethoven, Seven Bagatelles, Op. 33, No. 7

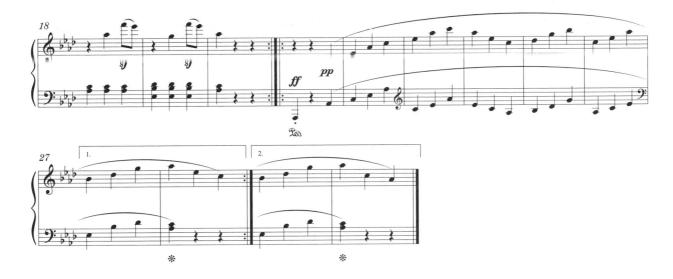

6. Steffani, "Französische Ouvertüre," mm. 1–32

Worksheet 41

Transcribing for Student Orchestras

Orchestrate the following pieces for either or both of these ensembles:

a. Middle school orchestra

b. High school or other non-professional orchestras

- It is advised that a violin III part be given in case there are no violas.

- Similarly, a possible clarinet or cello part would be useful in case oboes and bassoons are absent in the ensemble.

- If you wish, you can create a miniature concerto out of one of these examples, which could feature a particular fine instrumentalist who may be a member of the ensemble.

1. **Haydn, String Quartet, Op. 76, No. 2, third movement, Minuet**

2. La Monnoye, "Patapan"

5. Villa-Lobos, "O ciranda, o cirandinha," from *Guia prático*

Listen and Score 31

Humperdinck, *Hansel and Gretel*, Overture, mm. 1–11

- Listen to the excerpt with the piano reduction as many times as necessary. Then notate what you hear in full score.

- After you have finished, compare your realization to a full score.

Listen and Score 33

Mussorgsky-Ravel, *Pictures at an Exhibition,* **"Gnomus," mm. 19–27**

- Listen to the excerpt with the piano reduction as many times as necessary. Then notate what you hear in full score.
- After you have finished, compare your realization to a full score.

Listen and Score 34

Mussorgsky-Ravel, *Pictures at an Exhibition,* **"Ballet of the Chickens in Their Shells," mm. 1–8**

- Listen to the excerpt with the piano reduction as many times as necessary. Then notate what you hear in full score.
- After you have finished, compare your realization to a full score.

Credits

Béla Bartók, "44 Duos." © 1933 Boosey & Hawkes, Inc. Copyright Renewed. Reprinted by permission of Boosey & Hawkes, Inc.

Béla Bartók, "Three Burlesques, Sz. 47." © 1944 Boosey & Hawkes, Inc. Reprinted by permission of Boosey & Hawkes, Inc.

Béla Bartók, "Concerto for Orchestra, Sz. 115." © 1946 by Hawkes & Son (London) Ltd. Reprinted by permission of Boosey & Hawkes, Inc.

Béla Bartók, "For Children, Sz. 42." © Copyright 1946 by Boosey & Hawkes Music Publishers Ltd. for the world excluding Germany, Austria, Hungary, Romania, Czech Republic, Slovakia, Poland, Bulgaria, Albania, China and the former territories of Yugoslavia and the USSR. Reprinted by permission of Boosey & Hawkes, Inc.

Aaron Copland, "Piano Variations." © 1932 The Aaron Copland Fund for Music, Inc. Copyright Renewed. Boosey & Hawkes, Inc., Sole Licensee. Reprinted by permission of Boosey & Hawkes, Inc.

Witalij Godsjatzky, "Risse der Flachen" (Surface Scratches). Copyright © 1968 by Musikverlag Hans Gerig Koln. Reprinted by permission.

Paul Hindemith, "Ludus Tonalis." Copyright © 1943 by Schott Music GmbH & Co. KG, Mainz, Germany. Copyright © renewed. All Rights Reserved. Used by permission of European American Music Distributors Company, sole U.S. and Canadian agent for Schott Music GmbH & Co. KG, Mainz, Germany.

Andrew Imbrie, "Serenade For Flute, Viola And Piano." Copyright © 1976 by Malcolm Music, a div. of Shawnee Press, Inc. Copyright Renewed. This arrangement Copyright © 2016 by Malcolm Music, a div. of Shawnee Press, Inc. International Copyright Secured. All Rights Reserved. Reprinted by permission of Hal Leonard Corporation.

Charles Ives, "The Last Reader." Copyright © 1933 by Merion Music, Inc. All rights administered by Theodore Presser Company. All rights reserved. Used with permission.

Tania Leon, "Ritual For Piano." Copyright © 1987 by Southern Music Pub. Co. Inc. This arrangement Copyright © 2016 by Southern Music Pub. Co. Inc. International Copyright Secured. All Rights Reserved. Reprinted by permission of Hal Leonard Corporation.

Bohuslav Martinu, "Quintette Pour Piano Et Cordes." Copyright © by Éditions Max Eschig. All rights reserved. Reproduced by kind permission of Hal Leonard MGB s.r.l. – Milan.

Modest Mussorgsky, "Pictures at an Exhibition" (arranged for full orchestra by Maurice Ravel). © Copyright 1929 by Hawkes & Son (London) Ltd. for All Countries of the World. Propriete en Co-edition Editions A.R.I.M.A. et Editions Boosey & Hawkes for the U.K., British Commonwealth, Eire, Germany, Austria, Switzerland, and the U.S.A. Reprinted by permission of Boosey & Hawkes, Inc.

Andre Previn, "Five Pages from My Calendar." © Copyright 1976 by Boosey & Hawkes Music Publishers, Ltd. Reprinted by permission of Boosey & Hawkes, Inc.

Maurice Ravel, "Miroirs n° V. La Vallée des cloches." Copyright © 1906 by E. Demets. Éditions Max Eschig, Paris – France. All rights reserved. Reproduced by kind permission of Hal Leonard MGB s.r.l. – Milan.

Wallingford Riegger, "Tone Clusters (from 12 Piano Pieces with Analytical Notes)." Copyright © 1945 by Boosey & Hawkes, Inc. Reprinted by permission of Boosey & Hawkes, Inc.

Arnold Schoenberg, "Kleines Klavierstuck." Courtesy of Belmont Music Publishers, Los Angeles.

Index of Works